Left

by

Stefanie Hutcheson

This is a work of fiction. Names, characters, places and incidents either are products of the author's imagination or are used fictitiously. Any resemblance to actual events or locales or persons, living or dead, is entirely coincidental.

For Steve.

*Although I tend to be the one in the driver's seat,
we both know it's you who keeps us
headed in the right direction.
Just make sure the tank stays filled!*

Table of Contents

Left

by

Stefanie Hutcheson

Day One

Did she really just do that? Did she really put the car in drive and while he went inside to pay, did she really take off? Not in a hurry, nor screeching the tires. Just drove on as though he was still beside her.

She didn't even look back. Didn't stop at the red light and turn around to go get him and say, "Ha ha! Gotcha!" And still, while she had one more opportunity before hitting the interstate, she didn't come to her senses, turn around, and apologize.

Or had she come to her senses?

She really didn't know what had gotten into her. She only knew that when she got to the offramp she saw a woman with the saddest eyes she had ever seen. She didn't know what she was so unhappy about. She wondered what had gone on in her life that made her cry so and then she realized: she was looking in the rearview mirror.

Day Two

He awakened the next morning, Saturday, to an empty bed. Thinking she must be in the kitchen fixing breakfast or some other household chore, he stretched lazily, checked the time, and then got up to use the bathroom. As he reached for his toothbrush, he remembered: it was in his shaving kit bag. Which was inside of his suitcase. Which was...where, exactly?

He'd stood outside of the gas station yesterday, waiting for her little prank to come to its hilarious conclusion. But after an hour or so, he realized the joke was on him. Plus the attendee was starting to look at him a bit strangely so he shrugged it off, inhaled an angry breath, and began the three-mile trek back to his house, stomping the first mile or so.

Good thing I always carry my set of keys. At least I'll be able to get in the house.

Thirty minutes later he arrived, fully expecting her car to be in the drive. It was not in the driveway (he had wondered if perhaps she had gotten sick and had had to make a mad dash home and that's why she left him at the station). He then made his way into the basement. But no: no silver Camry was there beside his Toyota Tundra. Nonetheless, as he made his way upstairs, he had called out her name.

No answer.

Fast forward to this morning. Trying her phone again, he heard her sing-song voice telling the caller she was off on her next great adventure, be sure to leave a message, and she'd call back when she could.

Honey? Where are you? I waited for you at the gas station but…

I am at home, in case you wondered. This might have been said a bit heatedly yet with just a touch of teasing in his voice. *Don't tell me you went on vacation without me!*

Suddenly at a loss for words, he ended the message with these words: *Call me. You know my number.*

Yesterday, he thought surely she'd have had her fun and would be back to get him. They'd start their trip over--but this time, by golly, *she* would be the one to pump the gas!

He made his way down to the basement--again--to see if her car was there. Maybe she came home, exhausted, and fell asleep in it.

She hadn't.

He checked his phone--again--to see if she had called and he'd slept through it.

He hadn't.

Tempted to call 911 and report her as missing, he slowed down to punt, to regroup. As he sat on that hard wooden basement step, he tried to remember what the name of the hotel was that they were going to stay at. She always handled the details so precisely that he rarely paid attention to the minute, instead fixating on the plans he'd made to entertain them. That's how it worked: she took care of the business end while he concentrated on the fun stuff. It had always worked before. Right?

Realizing that her special care for doing her part most likely meant she had their travel itinerary typed and/or written neatly out, he bounded up the stairs and went into the study. Sure enough, right beside her jar of Peanut Butter M&Ms, was the agenda.

Paradise Awaits was the resort's name. Time of expected arrival, room number, and the concierge's personal phone number were written in neat block letters, along with the confirmation and credit card numbers used to pay for the week's stay.

Taking his cell from his front pocket, he dialed the number for 'Leslie.' Not sure if this was a man or woman, he waited to be answered, planning along how best to get some information without sounding like a quack.

Five minutes later, he hung up.

'Leslie' had been most helpful, wondering if there was something wrong with their suite, and if so, what could she do to make it better. At least that was one question that got answered: 'Leslie' was a woman. The information she provided to him, however, only added more to his growing list of topics.

As she chattily described how she'd left the refrigerator stocked with all of his favorite beer (*Heineken, right?*) and hoped she'd gotten the right cheeses, crackers, and such that his wife had pre-ordered, Leslie wondered if they had slept well. She knew from her records that the check-in had gone smoothly and was so sorry that she hadn't been there to personally greet them but a family emergency had kept her tied up.

After assuring her they had everything they needed, he was able to break off the call. As he hung up, he sank in his wife's chair, completely baffled. It was apparent that she was there.

Paradise Awaits. The brochure seemed to mock him.

Oh yeah? Then why do I feel like I am in hell?

Day Three

Sunday. Church day. Would he go? *Should* he go? Usually, he taught every other week in the married couples' class. Since their vacation had been arranged--theoretically--weeks ago, his place was covered.

He debated within himself how much *he* might need some counseling at church. But, did he really want to get into explaining why he was there alone and face all the questions? He could almost hear them now:

- *Where's your better half?*
- *She* left *you at the gas station? What kind of wife does that?*
- *So, let me get this straight. For the past decade you have been preaching to us how to keep our marriages afloat when yours was the one sinking?*

Picking up the phone, he checked to see if there were any messages. Maybe she had forgotten her charger. Maybe two nights without him had given her the time for--for whatever it was she needed to think about. Maybe she was heading home!

Excitedly, he punched in his passcode and saw that he had three missed calls. Unfortunately, none were from his wife. His mom had left a message saying she needed a ride to the chiropractor on Wednesday. Then she remembered he was off "honeymooning" and to "never mind." She'd ask someone else. Reminding him to be sure to wear his sunscreen, she gaily crooned the lyrics to "Under the Boardwalk" before ending her message.

The other two calls were unimportant. Between his student loans and his car warranty notifications that were nonexistent, he had no one else who checked up on him so much.

Except her. Every day they'd call one another, to reassure the one that the other had gotten to work or wherever unscathed, to remind that dinner was at Mama Louise's this week, or just to say "I love you."

He stared at the phone in his hand. Slowly he punched in her number. Holding his breath, he waited for her to pick up. Her answering machine repeated the same information it had the day before.

"Hi! I can't talk to you right now because my love and I are on a top secret mission. Leave a message...if you dare!

Dare he? It'd been two nights and…

Beep!

His time to speak had run out. Staring at her picture on his screen, he touched her face. She smiled back at him. The call disconnected. He wondered how they had done so too.

Day Four

He came home to an empty house. He'd always enjoyed quiet but this? This wasn't really what he had in mind. This quiet was different. This quiet was so loud it seemed to shout, "She's gone!"

As he walked to the bathroom to take his blood pressure pill before supper, just as he had done for countless years before, he realized there wouldn't be any supper. He sniffed the air to be sure. His stomach growled in protest and he sighed, took a leak, and washed his hands. He stared at the bottle before opening it up to take that tiny pink pill. He considered taking two because his blood pressure was really climbing these days.

Making his way to the kitchen, he called out her name. Maybe she was in the other bathroom and hadn't heard him come in. Once again the silence shouted back at him, the same as before. The quiet was the only response he got.

Day Five

Tuesday. She usually met with a group of ladies on Tuesdays for a Bible Study, lunch, and--depending on the weather--either a long walk or a game of tennis.

The lessons they had been studying had been about the sanctity of marriage. It was an offshoot, of sorts, from their Sunday School class. Mark 10:9 was their verse: *What therefore God hath joined together, let not man put asunder.*

Because their church was a large one, new folks frequently joined. The "mature" ladies had been partnered up with newlyweds, to assist them in the transition from being single to couplehood. They called this group "Sisters" and they met once a month for a ladies-only fellowship. But on Tuesdays, she and some others met to do a more in-depth study so that they could better themselves, first, before sharing their wisdom with the ones who might need some mentoring.

The past few weeks had been spent discussing many of the ways that the world tried to tear apart couples. From adultery to idolatry, nothing was left off of the table.

Except for when a woman leaves her husband at the gas station for reasons no one can explain.

Was she having a mental break? She must be, for what on earth could possibly allow for her to leave her husband to fend for himself while she carelessly left him behind?

Dear God! What have I done?!

She walked over to the balcony and laughed out loud, thinking she was just as crazy as that woman in the middle of the ocean in this fifty-degree weather.

Some role model I am!

At least she had the sense--or so she told herself--to come in from the cold.

Nonetheless, she shivered as she pulled her arms more tightly around herself for warmth. The chill in her heart, however, seemed colder each day.

Day Six

He woke up hungry, alone, and with another base desire that led to his disposition being less than sunny.

As he looked at the empty space in the bed--their bed--he did something he rarely did. He swore. He punched his pillow and for good measure, threw hers off of the bed. It hit her nightstand, and knocked their picture off. It didn't break, but his heart shattered as he recalled when it was made.

The summer of 2008. "The Year of Celebration" she had called it, because it symbolized that they had been married for twenty-five years.

The kids had gotten together and arranged a surprise party for them. After eating and being roasted (he wasn't sure which offspring of his had had this wonderful idea but was pretty sure it was their son), gifts and cards had been presented. One in particular stood out. Addressed only to his beloved, the front of it said "In deepest sympathy."

He watched as she tried to hide the card, as well as the tears that had changed from happy to sad ones.

Because he knew her so well, he spilled his drink to take the attention off of her. Yeah, it ruined his favorite golf shirt, but what was that compared to his wife's happiness?

Later, as they went outside to enjoy the warmth of the evening, pictures were made of them with all of their friends in various poses. Wishing he had known beforehand of this event, he had no gift to give his partner. Thankfully, their granddaughter was fond of quarter machines and had purchased several cheap candy necklaces and bracelets and rings. She slipped over to him, made him lean down so she could whisper in his ear, and placed her sticky hand into his. Giving her a conspiratorial wink, he made his way over to his wife, dropped down to one knee, and asked her if she'd kindly do him the honor of marrying him--again--for another twenty-five years. She pretended to ponder it a moment, and as he extended the rainbow marble-colored ring, held out her hand while excitedly proclaiming she most certainly would.

It was that moment that was captured in the picture now lying on the floor, out of his sight but seared into his mind.

Oh darling! You promised! We still have thirteen more years to go.

Why did you leave?

Getting out of bed and pushing the covers to the side, he made his way over to the photograph. Holding it in his hand, checking to make sure it hadn't cracked, he traced her face. He ran his hand down her arm, to her hand, where the ring was being placed on her finger. She was radiant! The sun's glow made her look as though she was in the spotlight. Her eyes…

Damn it! Damn damn damn it!

He slammed the picture, face down, back in its place. Heading to the shower, he busted his toe on the bed's frame. Howling in pain, hobbling to the chair to examine it, and waiting for her to come running to see what was the matter, he remembered once again: she wasn't there. Instead of the anger he had awakened with, he now only felt sadness.

Come back. Come home.

Day Seven

"You'd better not start any shit!"

Car door slammed, but for reiteration purposes, the man menacingly hissed it at his passenger again, throwing in another unkind label as she got out on the other side.

Totally oblivious to me parked beside him, he went from Mr. Hyde to Dr. Jeckyl in an instant. Jerking his door open and carelessly smacking it into my passenger-side door, he leaned in. Lovingly, he helped his small daughter from her car seat, as he gently cooed for her to hang on and to be sure to grab Daddy's hand.

The woman, head bowed low, tried to make herself invisible as she helped their son out of his car seat. Placing a swift kiss on his head, she closed the door gently.

The four of them walked across the parking lot and entered the dollar store. None saw me, as I alternated between anger at how he spoke to her then to fear that he might be easily set off was I to interrupt to tell him that was no way to talk to anyone--much less the mother of his children. Nor any other human being for that matter.

I sighed within myself, wondered if this was her daily lot in life. Made me think about if mine was really so bad after all.

Day Eight

She couldn't believe she was still here. Thankfully, at this time of the year, the hotel rates were manageable so she arranged to stay another week.

Another week?

As she strolled along the beach, watching the dolphins frolic from a distance, she couldn't help but wonder what he was doing now.

4:30. He's at work, too busy to give her any thought. But soon it would be time for him to clock out and go home. Would he have something healthy for supper or would he stop at a fast-food joint? Did he have clean clothes?

She had done the laundry before their trip but because he had to wear work shirts, he was probably on his last one. And the milk, bread, and eggs would have run out by now, assuming he fixed breakfast for himself.

A jogger nearly ran into her interrupting her reverie, and quickly apologized. Noticing the darkening of the sky, she turned around and headed back up the beach. It would soon be time to call it a day and what did she have to show for it?

Nothing.

She had spent the last week basically doing nothing. No cooking. No cleaning. No laundry. No bill paying, grocery buying, and certainly not any conversing. Alone with her thoughts and trying to figure out how she could have walked away so easily, most of her days had been spent on the balcony. Or couch while she played mindless computer games. On afternoon walks where she tried to let her chaotic thoughts be chased away by the coastal breezes.

So far, it wasn't working.

Day Nine

"Hey Daddy! I've been trying to get in touch with Mom but I just keep getting her voice mail."

"Huh. Wonder what's up with that?" It was the first thing he could think of to say.

"Yeah, well, I kind of need her advice. Is she there?"

Uh oh. What should I do?

"Earth to Dad. Can you please put Mom on the phone? I really need to talk to her!"

Their youngest daughter was always in some sort of drama and it usually involved her roommate, prissy dog, or latest hairstyle. Not that she was flighty. But sometimes he wondered how she had missed out on the common sense that her older siblings had in abundance.

Not wanting to lie but not knowing what the truth was either, he tried to steer their youngest into another direction, making a remark about how he himself was pretty good at doling out advice, why not ask him. But she misunderstood his tone and said, "Ooh, I'm not interrupting something, am I?" She broke into a giggle, totally believing that her parents were enjoying their recent empty nest.

"Well..." he said slyly, "as a matter of fact, we were just..."

"No, Dad. Gross! I don't want any details! Ick. You two just go ahead and do...well, whatever it is you are doing. Tell Mom I'll call her in a couple of days or she can call me. Oh, and have her check to make sure her phone's charged.

"Take care, Daddy. Love you!"

She hung up as he was saying "I love you too, honey."

Staring at the phone in his hand, he sighed before dialing the number he knew by heart. Sure, he could have just clicked on her picture but for some reason it made his eyes tear up to see his wife's smiling face while his own had tears streaming down it.

Day Ten

She shivered and hugged herself tightly, even though today was one of those wonderful fall days where the sun was brilliant, the breeze warm, and the reflection of the sun against the ocean blinding.

Had she really been here nine days? She shook as the cold enveloped her once more. Clutching her sweater more securely around her arms, she wondered why her hands were shaking. Was this normal? It must be seventy-five degrees out here on the hotel's veranda.

Maybe I am coming down with something.

She felt her forehead to see if she could feel heat from a possible fever.

No. Her head and cheeks felt normal. As she returned to her book that she had brought out to take her mind off of him, she couldn't seem to stop them from shaking. They were so cold she felt like they'd break if one was moved wrongly.

Frowning again, she got up to walk around, to see if the movement would get her blood flowing. Avoiding eye-contact with other vacationers, her attention was drawn to the ones who dared to brave the ocean. It had been a tempestuous summer, with a record number of hurricanes. All sorts of critters and debris had been stirred up in the Atlantic and there was no way she was going to swim in its convoluted mess.

The chill in her heart seemed to mock her as it echoed "critters," "debris," and "tempestuous." The iciness inside of her only hardened as she contemplated how she had so callously left her husband behind at the gas station. Surely no woman in her right mind would do what she had done.

As she examined these thoughts, she tried to make order of them and what caused the break--for something had definitely been broken. Cracked. Fractured. And now those frozen fractals were piercing her heart and mind. She would add "soul" but at this point, she wondered what had become of hers.

Day Eleven

"Six, please."

The man politely pushed the elevator button for me, as he ushered his partner to the side. Two other folks were also getting on and as the lady started to inquire what floor they needed, he gave a gentle touch to her back, reminding her that he was in charge, and her job was to be quiet. She hung her head, readjusted her smile, and stayed out of the way.

As I got off on the sixth floor and went back to my room, I recalled times I myself had been shushed and gently prodded underneath the table to stop talking or to refrain from any further discussion on the matter that was at hand. After all our years together, he still had not quite gotten used to the fact that I could control my tongue on my own. He saw it as being helpful and I? I saw it as a sign of mistrust.

Day Twelve

Tuesday. His night to go out with the fellas and to have supper before going to the bowling alley. He'd already packed his ball, gloves, and shoes. He didn't need permission to go and determined he was still going to face life head-on. After all, did he really have a choice?

His phone calls had gone unanswered. Straight to voicemail and after the first ten days, he stopped leaving messages.

He wasn't worried about her in a general way. Tracking her whereabouts was easy. *Thanks, Alexa.* She was at a hotel that they hadn't stayed at before and Bank of America was kind enough to let him know when there were transactions over a hundred dollars. A few days ago, he got the notification on his phone that she had extended her stay for another week.

The neighbors didn't seem to notice her absence, which was good. It was hard enough at work trying to explain why there weren't any peanut butter crackers each day.

She used to make him a bagful each morning--with plenty to share with the other guys. Making a joke about his diet being tightly controlled now, he brushed off their remarks without letting on in the least that he had been left. They told him they weren't on a diet; she could still send some in for them.

Left.

Odd word.

Did it mean discarded, forgotten, or done with? Finished and no longer needed? All that remains?

He wasn't sure but at this point, he was sick of thinking about it. Besides, he was going to get his first real meal since the gas station incident. A fourteen-ounce ribeye should do the trick!

Day Thirteen

As she laid there in the silence, she marveled at its intensity. All those evenings spent repeating herself because he wasn't really listening. All the times he did hear but didn't listen. Why she bothered, day in, day out to keep trying to converse with him was...not a mystery. More of a habit.

As in the distance she heard guests in the hall, waiting for the ping of the elevator, she pondered how much of her time she had spent listening. Waiting for his key to click in the lock, footsteps creaking on the floor, morning noises men make as they awaken. Listening for his response to her questions. Listening for his voice to gauge what kind of day he had. Hearing the tiredness or the frustration. Occasionally hearing his tone change when he needed special attention.

It was quiet here. The peacefulness had made her edgy at first, because she feared being found. Even though she wasn't lost, after all this time, she wondered if she was even missed.

The silence spoke volumes.

Day Fourteen

She needed to make a decision. The front-desk kept calling to see if she was going to be checking out or staying with them a few more days. It wasn't as though they needed her room. Not at this time of year. No, they were just being solicitous.

She glanced around the room and did a quick inventory. She had only packed for a week's stay and while the hotel had a laundry service, it was getting cooler. The clothing packed was for early fall and its promise of warm temperatures. However, the weather pattern shifted and a cold front had settled in.

She walked over to the suitcase, still lying on the extra queen bed. They always got a room with two beds because she never knew if her restlessness would keep him awake at night. While she had arranged her clothing in the provided dresser of the hotel, his was still in the suitcase.

She unzipped it and picked up one of his shirts and held it to her face. She breathed in his essence and suddenly ached for him so badly she could hardly stand. Clutching the garment, she remembered their discussion when packing for the trip.

He had tried to tell her that it would be too hot and he didn't need this sweater. She countered with how pretty it made his eyes look and besides, on all of their late-night walks, he'd need something to keep him warm. Grinning mischievously at her, he had reached for her and drew her into an embrace. "That's what I've got you for!" Shooing him off, she declared there'd be plenty of time for that while they were away.

As she pulled the sweater over her head, she sighed, wishing it was his arms enfolding her instead of the lined flannel Columbia jacket's lifeless ones.

Day Fifteen

Well, I guess that answers that.

The notification came in last night from the bank. Another charge was made to the hotel. Comparing it from last week's amount, she had decided to make it another week without him.

By now he was well aware of her habits. On Mondays (according to the bank statement) she ordered pizza from the Pizza Hut. Wednesdays she went to Publix Super Market at Village Shops at Grande Dunes. There was a trip to a nail salon--something she rarely did but must have decided to treat herself. He recollected how once a month he used to give her a pedicure and how, gosh...how long had it been? He used to rub her feet weekly and lotion them and try to tickle her while she fought to not laugh out loud. She hated to lose control and felt that when he mercilessly made her squeal she was giving up a piece of herself that she would rather have hung onto.

Other than a few other charges to places such as Krispy Kreme (he was sure she would have gotten the chocolate iced), a trip to Walmart (probably for a change or two of clothing, he thought, as he adjusted the thermostat. He knew the beach was having a cold spell and didn't remember whether or not she had packed accordingly), along with the morning jaunts to Starbucks, she didn't appear to be spending much.

Speaking of which, he probably should stop for a few groceries himself. The refrigerator was looking pretty sparse and he'd run out of peanut butter. And crackers. Somehow he found an odd comfort in making them for supper each evening.

Day Sixteen

Saturday. Another weekend alone.

What should I do? Go to Myrtle Beach, grab her by the hair of her head, and drag her back home with me? Leave her there until she comes to her senses? What if she never comes to her senses?!

Should I cut off her credit cards, declare her as incompentent and have the police hold her until I can get her admitted into a psychiatric hospital? Should I have a tow-truck confiscate her Camry and tell them it was stolen?

As he considered his options, he heard that familiar beep that notified him he had a message. Anxiously he reached for the Samsung and then cursed as it fell to the ground. Usually mild-mannered, he marveled as once again he was made aware of how short his fuse was these days.

Great. That's just great.

He stared at the phone's screen that was now instead a fractured piece of equipment. It made him feel like he was in an M. Night Shyamalan movie. But instead of seeing dead people, he only saw a shattered screen that reminded him of their life that she had wrecked.

Day Seventeen

There she was again. How she could stand being in the chilly waters of the Atlantic was a mystery. For the past three days, I witnessed her as she witnessed to me.

Hands raised, words unheard, she was vigorously conversing. Arguing at times, or so it seemed. It was as though she had gained an audience with the king and was making each second count.

I continued to watch her. She mesmerized me.

She turned around. Our eyes met. And held. I shivered, not sure what was going on. Suddenly my heart began to beat rapidly. I wanted to run, but it was as though my feet were cemented into the sand. I couldn't look away--and she certainly wasn't going to. Holding my gaze, she began walking towards me.

As though of their own accord, my feet started walking towards her. In seconds, we were facing each other. Eyes still locked, neither of us made a sound. My heart began to still. My breathing relaxed. Time stood still as we, two strangers, read each other's life stories, read each others' souls in the span of a moment.

Finally, although no words were spoken by either of us, she blinked. The most brilliant smile I had ever seen broke forth across her face. Then, she laughed. Big, belly-shaking guffaws of laughter oozed from this woman and I wasn't sure what my response should be.

After a couple of minutes, she regained control of herself. Giving me one last long look, she walked back into the sea. I thought I heard her say "Good one, Lord."

She resumed her waist-high stance in the ocean and kept her conversation going. Once, she looked behind to see if I was still there. With a slight wave, she turned, raised her hands toward heaven, and I? I slowly walked back to the hotel, carrying within me the story I needed to hear.

Day Eighteen

I wasn't in the best of moods. Sleep had eluded me all night as I restlessly stirred throughout the night. My job. My home. My wife. A constant barrage of unanswered questions.

I dreamt I was in a dark place, maybe an alley--although I had rarely been in one before. While there was little light to illuminate, something about this place was familiar. As I made my way down towards the other end, something was trying to get my attention. Not a voice; not something I could name. But yet, there was a force of some sort that wanted me to find it, to rescue it, to set it free.

I rummaged through some boxes, checked to see if any of the doors to the building were unlocked. They weren't. I grabbed my cell phone and used its night light feature, but it wasn't charged. However, when I felt in my pocket, there was a note there, the message fading away as I desperately tried to read it. I couldn't make out the words!

Running to the other end of the block, I sought for an open bar, grocery store, anything that might have electricity and a means of charging my battery long enough for me to read those few words. But everything was closed. Not even a neon sign was flashing.

A dog barked. Someone hollered for it to shut up. Then it yelped, as though it had been kicked. I never could stand for animal abuse and my eyes wandered along the building face to see if I could determine where the sounds came from.

But it was dark. Black. Everything was black.

Day Nineteen

He left the Verizon store, new phone intact. Even though he had gotten a quick lesson on how it worked, he sure wished he could have one of his grandchildren to walk him through it.

He opened it and was surprised to see that his home screen looked pretty much the same as his old one.

Maybe this won't be so bad, after all.

As he scrolled through the icons, he zoned in on his messenger app. Hope surged through his heart when he saw that there were four--four!!--new messages. Punching in his pass code, he impatiently sighed.

Welcome to Verizon. Thank you for joining our…

Delete.

Next message.

As a new Verizon customer, you have been specially selected to…

Delete.

Third message.

We've been trying to reach you concerning your extended car warranty…

His hopes were fading fast. Breathing a quick prayer, he listened to the final message.

Dad? Hey! I just wanted to check up on you and Mom. She hasn't returned any of my calls. I'm starting to get a little nervous.

Chuckle.

Please remind her that you guys said you'd keep the kiddos soon. The hubs and I really need a night out! Just like you guys taught us: keep the romance flowing.

Dad?

Voice more serious now.

Are you guys okay? Is Mom *okay? This isn't like her to not call me every week.*

Call me back, Dad. Love you.

He clicked to save her message and sighed. It was bad enough she wasn't speaking to him. But to make the girls worry?

Not good, honey.

He started to give her another call. The first few numbers he punched in brought up her profile pic.

Wow, these new phones are kinda scary. I didn't have to reprogram my contacts.

Shaking himself mentally from his reverie, he touched her face, just as he had done with the picture on the nightstand a couple of nights ago. Grimacing, he hit the connect button and listened once more to her telling the caller she was sorry she couldn't talk now.

He started to hang up, longing for the old days when one could slam the receiver down. However, remembering the purpose of his call, he left her with the command to call their daughters--both of them. They were worried about their mom, as was he.

It's the least you can do.

He wanted to say more but didn't trust himself at this point. So, instead, he ended the call, saying "By the way, I got a new phone today. Number's still the same. Just in case you want to give me a call."

Angry exhalation.

"Call me."

Day Twenty

Not knowing why and wondering just when--if ever--she was going back, she called the concierge and arranged to stay for another week. She got her car from the hotel's parking garage and made her weekly trip to Publix. They had the prettiest bouquet of sunflowers that she just had to have and for some reason, they made her smile. Though they had no scent, she buried her face in their beauty and sighed.

After purchasing another quart of milk, grabbing a bag of Ruffles, some Belvitas for breakfast, and another pack of ham for lunch--along with a couple of bananas, oranges, and cucumbers--she paused at the meat aisle.

That's a great price on London Broil! I should grab one and we'll be having my famous Mississippi Crock Pot Roast with some mashed potatoes for supper. Do we have potatoes in the freezer or should I grab a pack of Ore Idas?

Making her way to the freezer section, she suddenly remembered, once again: she wasn't home. There wasn't anyone in this hotel to cook for. Fighting the sensation she felt in her eyes, stumbling out of the store, leaving her groceries behind, and barely managing to get to her car, she promptly burst into tears.

When she regained herself, she reached in the console for a tissue. As she dabbed at her eyes in the rearview, she saw the woman from the ocean. Eyes full of pity, hands on her broad hips, she shook her head. Then--even though she wasn't wearing a watch--the woman looked at her left arm, signifying it was time for her to be somewhere.

A cloud broke free, sending down a blinding beam of light that reflected into her eyes, causing her to temporarily go blind. When she was able to adjust them, the woman was gone.

Putting her key into the ignition, she made her way back to the hotel. She knew what she needed to do.

Day Twenty-One

After watching the sun rise--a habit I had fallen in love with performing nearly each day since arriving--I made my way down to the lobby. The hotel had a Starbucks nearby and I was ready for my quiet time. While viewing the morning begin surely evoked peace, this was separate from my desire to commune with God through His Word.

I ordered my usual Vanilla Latte and made my way over to the chair and table near the window. Placing the drink to my left and taking a journal and Bible from my satchel, I realized I didn't have a pen. From out of nowhere, or so it seemed, instantaneously there was a pen being handed to me.

Looking up to see who was at the other end of the extended hand with the pencil proffered, I smiled immediately. It was the woman from the sea!

As I placed the writing utensil beside my notebook, I wondered if I should invite her to sit. But when I looked up, she was gone.

Hours later, coffee long reordered and drunk, journal filled with many thoughts, I realized the time. Not that I had anywhere to be but also knowing that an appointment of another variety needed to be kept.

When back at the resort, I frenetically pushed the elevator buttons, stabbing them over and over as though this would help it to arrive at my floor any faster. Dropping the keycard in my excitement to get inside, I nearly screamed in frustration as I heard my phone ringing. Finally I heard the blessed click signifying that I could enter.

I rushed over to the table by the couch, painfully bumping my knee into it as I grabbed for my cell. Hobbling over to sit, I saw his number as the missed call. With great anticipation, I waited for the voice mail, longing to hear him tell me he was at lunch and was just checking in as he'd done for the past thirty plus years. But no following beep came. Just empty silence.

The new ordinary.

Day Twenty-Two

It was nearly 6:00 pm. He should have been clocked out at 5:00 but a customer came in at the last moment. Knowing the other fellas had homes, lives--and wives--to get to, he volunteered to stay and take care of him. After all, what was the hurry?

Stopping at the grocery store, he got a plate from the deli. Then he decided he might be hungry this weekend so he grabbed some extra chicken legs, potato wedges, and green beans. Passing the bakery, he noticed the array of pound cakes. Remembering how she would make chocolate sauce or dice up some strawberries to go on top, he grabbed one and put in the buggy.

This will surprise her! Of course, no one can make a dessert like she can. I hope she won't be thinking that I prefer store-bought to her home cooking!

And that's when the little voice inside his head mocked him and told him she wouldn't. Asking it why, it seemed as though the demon laughed.

Oh yeah. You're right, little guy. She won't mind at all.

Angrily pushing his cart to the side, he stormed out of the store. It wasn't until later that night, when his belly reminded him that they hadn't eaten, that he called Domino's. Recognizing his number, the attendant on the phone asked him if he wanted his usual. As he stared at the empty pizza boxes around him that he had let pile up, he agreed. After all, did it even matter anymore?

Day Twenty-Three

After he finished mowing the yard, he put in a load of laundry. Noticing the ever-expanding pile of pizza boxes, he gathered them, along with the empty drink cans, and bagged them up. Collecting the few dishes, he washed them and put them up. Then he went to take a shower.

Naked, he stood in front of the mirror. He examined himself closely as he applied the shaving cream to his face.

I could use a hair cut.

The face looking back at him did not respond.

In fact, the silence was deafening. Reaching over to do something he rarely--if ever--did, he turned on the radio. Something she always did. He smiled, as he recollected how he'd catch her singing in the shower when she thought he was in the garage tinkering. He'd quietly listen and then when she turned the water off, he'd be waiting there with a towel for her to step in to. Her squeal delighted him to no end as she smacked at him for startling her.

48

Arms enveloped around her, he'd throw her over his shoulder and haul her off to the bedroom. She'd pretend she had other things to do, that she didn't have time for this, but her protests were weak.

He grabbed the nearby towel, hoping to catch her scent still lingering in it. Instead, he groaned. *What was that stench?*

Tossing it far from him, that face in the mirror laughed at him. Catching its eye, he smiled back. He wasn't sure why. But something was different. As he turned the shower on, Kelly Clarkson belted out "What Doesn't Kill You Makes You Stronger." As she boldly claimed about standing taller, being a fighter, and not being alone, he joined in. He muddled through the words and butchered them horribly, but this chick anthem gave him a release that helped him to realize that he too was not going down without a fight.

Day Twenty-Four

She scrolled through her Facebook Memories. She smiled as she saw the Scarecrow and Dorothy handing out trick-or-treat candies to the kids at the annual hospital fall festival. She recalled how they had always donned costumes from movies. The next picture showed, from eight years ago, the two of them dressed up as Olaf and Elsa.

The children's hospital had gone all out for the *Frozen* theme, and they had worked several nights on making marshmallow treats for the kids that resembled Olaf. The photo album from Facebook showed various pics of them but the one that caught her attention the most was when he was stuffing his mouth with more marshmallows than she could count. Beside him were two kids, doing the same. They were laughing and making an unrestrained sight as she remembered telling them to smile and say "Boogers!" They had tried to contain those marshmallows but, overcome by giggles, they tumbled out of their mouths.

She recalled loving his easy way with kids. He seemed to have a knack for making them feel safe, telling them the scars from their surgeries were actually tattoos that showed the world that they were fierce warriors. Weaving tales of fantasy to encourage the ones from the burn units, he made fables of how they had been through the fire and were indestructible. The wrinkled and red skin? It was really so that the world wouldn't know they were superheroes in disguise. Their true identities must be protected! Until that day of complete healing, they must do whatever it takes to not let anyone find out.

Ahh honey. You were such a good man. Are such a good man!

She continued scrolling but was interrupted by her phone ringing. Soon after letting it go to voicemail, she heard a buzzing noise, letting her know she had a new message.

She didn't have to check to see who it was from. His face had instantly appeared and the ringtone signified it was him. Pulling his shirt around her, longing to hear his voice, she hesitated before pushing the play button.

What am I afraid of? Why do I keep ignoring him? It isn't fair.

51

She had done much soul-examining these past weeks. Yet…yet she wasn't ready. She wasn't ready to go back. Wasn't sure she wanted to, in all honesty. Their marriage was a good one, no doubt. But...but lately something seemed to have changed. Call it complacency, routine, or...or...*nice*, their marriage had become staid. Same ol' same ol, day in and day out. After thirty-seven years, wasn't there supposed to be more?

She decided she didn't want to think about it anymore right now. Heading over to the balcony, she looked and, sure enough, that woman was at her usual post. She must have sensed her gaze, for she turned, gave a slight wave, and pointed to her left arm again where most people wore a watch. After tapping it a few times, she turned away and raised her arms again to the sky.

She hurried back inside and dropped to her knees. She prayed and cried and confessed to God what she was feeling, knowing He would make sense of her jumbled up words. Several moments later, she was spent.

She walked over to the desk to retrieve a tissue and saw the hotel stationery that was provided to send a postcard or jot down some things. Grabbing a card, she quickly began to write. It was the fourth time she'd written to him since she'd been at the resort. Holding the card in her hand, she quickly wrote a note.

Before she could reconsider, she rushed downstairs and asked the attendant to mail it for her. He offered her some more postcards, and at first she declined. When he cajoled her with a big smile once more, she accepted the items, thinking maybe she'd send the kids and grandkids a note, too. Thanking him, she meandered over to the lobby and began writing.

Might as well let them know I am okay.

And for the first time since leaving, she thought she almost was.

Day Twenty-Five

He was almost afraid to look at his phone this morning. The fear of seeing another charge to the hotel kept him from checking it before work as he usually did. Maybe if he didn't look, the hope that she would not be extending her stay could last for another little bit.

A man can dream, right?

Day Twenty-Six

Harmless flirting is rarely harmless. That was the topic he had taught in his Married Couples Sunday School Class two days ago. With much fervor, he had discoursed on marriage and its sanctity; how it is virtually impossible to be friends with someone of the opposite sex without the devil trying to sneak in and cause the slightest of temptations--at first--and then build into territory that could soon become dangerous.

So, while he drove home after work, an incident from earlier in the day pricked his consciousness. An attractive sales rep had come in. Not sure whether to be flattered or affronted--when her hand lingered on his as she handed him the contract to sign he felt...something. A tingle of sorts.

Do women just automatically sense when a man is being "neglected" at home? 'Cause this lady sure seemed to notice the little details that somehow show I am not getting my needs met.

While he didn't feel she was on the prowl, he felt that if given just a little encouragement, that she would be more than willing to meet after work. And, by golly, it'd been over three weeks since his wife left! What harm could come from a casual supper with this attractive woman who would provide him with some much-needed attention. Plus, he'd get a good meal out of it.

When her hand lingered on his, it had felt good--something he hadn't felt in a while. It wouldn't be a "date." Nope, just doing his part to keep the vendor/customer relationship friendly. And of course, dinner wasn't really what was on his mind.

As he turned into his driveway, he looked at himself in the rearview mirror and nearly gagged.

Hypocrite.

His own eyes accused him and the shame was great. So, when he absentmindedly ran into the mailbox, he vented his emotion on it instead.

"Freakin 'mailbox! You made me scratch my truck."

The mailbox, of course, did not respond although its door opened at the touch of the Tacoma against it. Several items, including sales papers, bills, and other correspondence fell out. Realizing he hadn't checked it in a while, he hastily got out of the truck and gathered the numerous papers. Stuffing them under his arm, he got back in the truck, pulled into the garage, and glared at the wall.

Not wanting to go into his empty home--as evidenced by the still bare spot next to his truck where her Camry should be--he rifled through the bills and felt angry again. He realized some of them probably hadn't been paid. The various grocery store papers with their tantalizing meats and breads he viciously wadded into a ball and threw aside. The postcards gleefully advertising "wish you were here" at *Paradise Awaits* nearly caused him to swear. There were three of them and he started to tear them in two when one with her handwriting caught his eye.

What the...? What's this?

As he read the neat handwriting of his wife while still reconciling in his mind that these weren't resort advertisements after all, he took a deep breath. Carefully holding the jagged edges of the cards in his hand and checking the postmarks on them, he realized something. She *had* been checking in with him weekly, after all. She hadn't been ignoring him:

she was reaching out the only way possible without causing a fight.

How stupid can I be? Of course she would have written. That was her way. Why didn't I think of that?

Reading them for a third and fourth time, something else was apparent. She was just as confused as he was about why she had left him behind. These words especially caught his attention:

> *What you did at the gas station before I drove off was the last straw. I didn't realize I had been counting them but... apparently--in my subconsciousness-- they had been adding up.*

Frantically searching his mind, trying to remember what happened that didn't normally happen each time they were together, he was at a loss. His eyes caught his reflection in the mirror again, mocking him this time.

Seriously, dude. You are going to play dumb here?

As he had done previously, he ignored that guy by viciously turning the mirror away from him, grabbed the mail, and shoved the truck's door a bit harder than necessary, causing another scrape to blend in with the one from the mailbox. Throwing the mail in a fit of fury, slamming the door, and--for good measure--kicking the tires, he sighed. And that's when his eyes lit on a fourth postcard. Somehow he had missed it.

Clutching it tightly to his chest, he hesitated before reading it. Somehow he felt that these words would change his life and he wasn't sure he was prepared for that. Dropping to his knees, he cried out to God for help. "Fix this!" he demanded.

After more prayer, he pleaded: "Fix me."

Soon, he stood. As he tried to shake the blood and feelings back into his feet and knees, he inhaled deeply, released it, and took the postcard inside. Sitting down at the kitchen table, he took one more breath, and began reading.

Day Twenty-Seven

"No. Thank you. While I have enjoyed my stay immensely, I will be checking out in the morning."

I'm ready to go back.

I think.

Deep breath.

I looked around the room. Yesterday I took advantage of the laundry service and so most of my clothes were clean. I'd been sleeping in his Columbia sweater and somehow didn't want it far from me--even if it was getting a slight smell to it.

My eyes lingered on his suitcase. I'd barely touched it but for some reason felt drawn to it this morning. Even though I had packed most of it, he had at the last moment thrown in a couple of items. Curiously, I decided to look through it.

Socks. Flip flops. Underwear. Swimming trunks and sleeveless t-shirts. Shaving kit. Shorts and a pair of sweats. His grey slacks and button-up blue shirt that made him look so professional. I ran my hand over the pleated pants, smoothing them out of habit as I did.

What was this?

There was something hard in the pocket.

A small box.

My heartbeat quickened.

Should I open it?

I looked around the room, as though being watched. Then I laughed nervously as I remembered there was no one to see.

Turning it this way, then that. Giving it a little shake to see if I could determine what was in there.

It was light. Jewelry, perhaps? I looked at my left hand at the diamond engagement ring with the wedding band keeping it snugly in place. Even though it had been thirty-seven years ago, I still remembered each word of the vow he had made to me.

I choose you to share my life with. For better and--with God's help--little worse. For richer, for poorer, in sickness and in health, I choose you and only you to be my awfully wedded wife.

He had laughed nervously here but with confidence as well because he knew if he didn't say it, I would have.

Then he had reached out his hand, gently but firmly taking me by the chin as I looked up into his sparkling blue eyes, and concluded.

"And death shall never part us. This is my solemn vow. From this moment on, I am yours. Will you have me?"

"Try and stop me" had been my response as the crowd laughed and the two of us kissed passionately before the preacher confirmed we were now pronounced man and wife.

With blurred eyes, I stared at the rings that confirmed the pledge we had made that day. Like a montage, memories of our life passed before me. So many good times! Three kids. Four homes. He'd been a good provider and indeed there had been little worse in their lives. He'd promised and he had kept his word.

Then why am I here now? Why had I mindlessly left him at the gas station nearly four weeks ago?

I marvelled at myself as these and a hundred and two other questions queried my brain.

Jumping from a sudden loud clap of thunder, my eyes were drawn to the window facing the ocean. The rain began to beat furiously at the open door and I hurried over to shut it before the floor got much wetter.

Too late.

Bashing my head into the corner of the living room table, I went down quickly on the slippery tiles. Dazed, I reached up to touch my head. When I brought my hand back down, it was covered in blood.

I tried to call out but the pain was blinding. My phone was on the kitchen counter, much too far away to be of any use. The raindrops swept in and I felt them and the blood both dripping down my face. And soon thereafter, I felt nothing.

Day Twenty-Eight

"Housekeeping. May I come in?"

No answer.

"Housekeeping! Can I come in" the voice asked, more exasperatedly.

Sighing to herself, she jiggled her master keys and put one into the door. Muttering to herself about having to pick up the slack and cover for those good-for-nothing lazy workers that had failed to show up today, she slammed the door a bit too hard as she entered, trying to fit her cart in as she angrily continued mumbling about not getting paid to do the work for three.

Instantly, she saw the suitcase on the bed and quickly began to apologize. Her back was to the room still and she hastily attempted to make her way out, saying she thought they had already checked out, so sorry, she'd come back later.

Reaching in front of her to open the door that had shut once she had rammed her cleaning cart through it, her eyes adjusted to the glow of the room. Although there weren't any lights on, the sun was brilliantly in high gear this morning, unlike the past couple of days when that unexpected storm had hit.

Apologizing once more for disturbing them, she glanced over her shoulder. There was a pigeon--no, two noisy pigeons!--on the kitchen counter in mid-flight from being disturbed from their feast of crackers from the opened package lying there.

"Get outta here, you crazy birds!"

She shooed them towards the window and that's when she noticed the heap on the floor. Clutching her cleaning cloth to her breast, she backed away, screaming.

"Oh my God! Oh my God! OH MY GOD!"

Day Twenty-Eight, pm

Coming to a screeching halt and almost bumping into the car in front of him, he slammed on his brakes, narrowly missing the hotel's outdoor waterfall. Quickly assessing the situation to make sure he hadn't inadvertently hit anyone, his view of the hotel was blocked by the family whose car he'd nearly crashed into. They were pushing and pulling the luggage car while at the same time, trying to make it, the baby's stroller, and the kids all move in the same direction.

So much for fifteen-minute parking to unload.

Frustrated beyond belief, he sat there agitatedly. Having driven all night and in a hurry to get to his wife, he was mad.

Mad over not knowing she'd write instead of calling.

Of course she would not stop communicating! Writing down her thoughts was her thing. I should have known her better!

Mad that he hadn't checked the mail sooner.

Why *didn't I check the mail sooner?*

Mad about the dents in his truck.

Mad she hadn't answered the phone even though he should have known better and she should have known him better. She knew how dense he could be. Sure, she wrote those postcards but come on: couldn't she have at least sent a text to remind him to check the mail?

Why *didn't they know each other better?*

As he had driven along the interstate to the coast, he had wrestled within himself all the ways he was going to be better. Enough with playing a role. While he hadn't realized they'd basically been playing house, this last month without her had shown him how shallow their marriage had become. His little chat with God the night before had enlightened him some. He was counting on her to do the rest.

So after driving all night, by the time he got to the hotel, he had only one thought on his mind. No more wasted time. No more excuses. No more deflection. From this moment on, they--*he*--was going to be different. Their golden years would be filled with less keeping up with the Joneses and more focus on each other.

If this family would just get out of my way!

He saw a parking spot across the street and quickly drove over to it. Darting across the road, he didn't see the ambulance parked to the side of the resort. It was in front of the car he'd nearly hit upon arrival.

Approaching the entrance, he locked eyes with a woman. She was staring intently at him with her hands on her hips.

Something about her gaze made him uneasy.

She seemed--with her eyes--to let him know he had failed and waited too long. Also, the look appeared to be combined with...pity? Sorrow? Rebuke?

Then, as if in slow motion, things started to happen. He broke off eye contact after she tapped her left arm, where a watch would be. She seemed to be admonishing him, which was definitely odd since he had never seen this woman before.

Shuddering, he broke off eye contact. Turning away from her, he started to make his way into the hotel's vestibule, dodging the family that still was struggling to get the luggage cart loaded. That was when he finally noticed the ambulance. Their dog was yipping at his heels and he was trying to shoo it away.

The hotel's doors began to open. A gurney was going to be loaded into the ambulance, and as the paramedics rolled it past him, he realized: it's too late. *I'm* too late.

Somehow he knew it was his wife under that white sheet.

No one seemed to notice him as he fell against the wall. The EMTs got into the van, turned off the flashing lights, and drove off. Just as had happened twenty-eight days ago, without any explanation, he had been left.

Made in the USA
Columbia, SC
13 July 2021